happiness is ...

happiness is ...

500 ways to show I love you

Lisa Swerling & Ralph Lazar

CHRONICLE BOOKS

SAN FRANCISCO

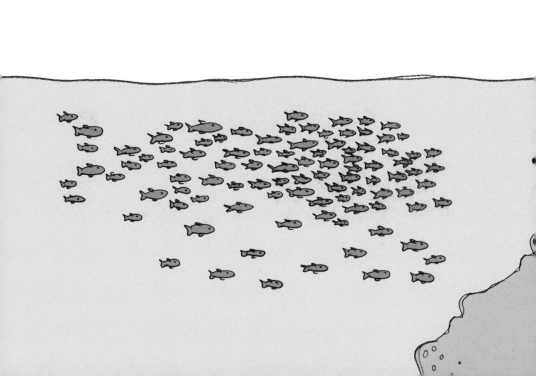

discovering new worlds

trusting you
completely

getting ready for the
day together

being the small spoon

being understanding

celebrating your success

getting my hair cut
the way you like it

being on the same side

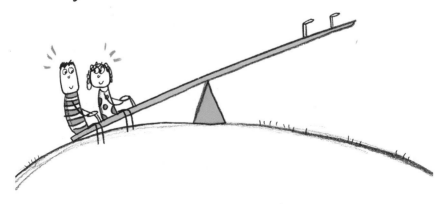

helping each other with
work-life balance

standing up for you

seeing the world through a similar lens

a kiss through
the phone

mapping out our life
together

looking at each other and
cracking up for no reason

sharing a sunset

finding our
dream home

SALE

appreciating your patience

talking late into the night

our stupid inside jokes

a laughter attack
for no reason

feeling excited when
your name pops up
on my phone

relaxing at the
end of a tiring day

hearing your voice

that electric touch

rushing out of work to meet you

Romeo & Juliet

being more excited about
your birthday than my own

escaping from
the crowd

tucking you in

facing the world together

sharing the good
and the bad

a sushi date

telling you you're beautiful

taking a risk because I'm with you

an unplanned date

getting a letter
from you

our engagement ring

pointing out little sweet things to each other

making the coffee
just how you like it

taking a great selfie
together

thinking of you
all the time

being cheek to cheek

never losing our
youthful glow

encouraging each other's creativity

being your partner in crime

teaching each other new
things

showing you that
I'm hilarious

our own secret recipes

you looking cute in
my sweater

splitting the
housework

just being
ourselves

sharing a meal outside

  buying you too many gifts

encouraging
your appetite

 packing for a trip together

realizing you're "the one"

feeling like an unbeatable team

being married to
your best friend

exploring new horizons

slow dancing

our special spot

knowing you're there for me

perfecting a super-annoying
wake-up routine

realizing how much I love you

appreciating your thoughtfulness

communication,
without words

driving for hours to see you

splurging on a
fancy hotel

sharing hobbies

making you smile

giggling in bed till late

getting lost on purpose

finding a book that reminds me of you

making a list of the
places we've traveled

being happy for you

watching the seasons change

when you lift me up
while hugging

writing a poem for you

discovering new places together

49

solving problems together

giving you a longer back
rub than you gave me

unwavering devotion

you and me and the
great outdoors

being inseparable

seeing your name in
my email inbox

stopping for junk food on a road trip

falling in love with a new city together

sleeping in your shirt

watching your
favorite movie for
the tenth time

being true to our childlike hearts

staying in love through it all

never saying "I told you so" even when I told you so

being on the same wavelength

realizing how
lucky we are

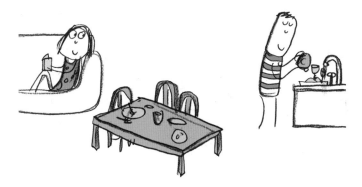

doing little favors for each other

waking up beside you

lying next to you in peaceful silence

surprising you with
flowers

giving you a push
when you need it

quiet weekday evenings

a sweet goodnight text

smiling stupidly because
a song reminds me of you

doing the dishes, even when it's your turn

watching the big game with you

making a wish about our future

treating ourselves

covering you up when
you fall asleep

remembering an
anniversary

Jack & Rose

finding our way

tickling you then running away

hearing your
heartbeat

romantic
gestures

knowing all of your best stories

scaring the living daylights out of you

humming along to one of our favorite songs

watching the clouds

rocking our bed heads

always making plans for our next vacation

a random wink

getting you the perfect gift

dreaming of you

finding our way back to each other

always saving
you a spot

having cute nicknames
for each other

getting butterflies
when I see you

when opposites
attract

watching you realize your dreams

spoiling you rotten

when your smile
makes everything ok

being ridiculous

listening to our song

when you grab my hand

decluttering to make
room for what's important

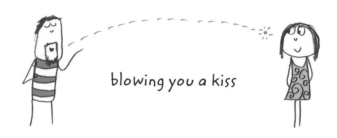

blowing you a kiss

giving you the heart
of my artichoke

simple coexistence

letting you show off

sleeping under the stars

being joined at the hip

79

having our own
definition of sanity

planning for
our future

believing in you,
always

letting our
hearts lead us

making your
favorite snack

when you look after me in
awkward social situations

making memories

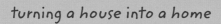

turning a house into a home

being alone together

letting go

acting like an idiot
to cheer you up

your little
snoring noises

enjoying the simple
moments

an indoor picnic

working side by side

having a shared mission

ADVENTURE

sneaking out of the party

waking up in
your arms

finding calm waters with you

being perfect
travel companions

sharing an unforgettable view

building something amazing together

appreciating
your cooking

exploring
together

being your chauffeur

tolerating your
eccentricities

DEPARTURES

breaking the rules

a romantic candlelit dinner for two

being in it
together

just us and the open road

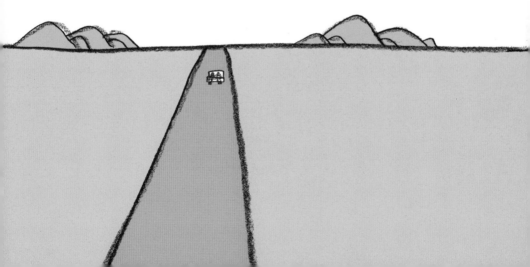

letting the little
things go

catching our dinner

one glass, two straws

knowing I have the best
partner of all

reading together
in a quiet house

getting our first pet

you popping onto
my desktop

learning your recipes

trying new things with you

becoming parents

humoring you when you're
lost but won't admit it

carving our first
pumpkin together

a long autumn stroll

a kiss chase

finding shelter

disregarding consequences

getting on a plane to see you

sharing a home

helping you chase your dreams

an empty beach and us

being on the ride of our lives

fantasizing about our
dream home

relaxing by the fire

our family traditions

breaking into
a random race

weathering storms together

you, me, and the cats

loving our crazy family

making you a cup
of tea just when
you need it

playing around like kids

watching hours of tv with you

introducing you to all my friends

two of us,
one piece of cake

teasing you

being given space
when you need it

being impressed by
how cool you are

a little healthy competition

a lazy weekend together

feeling fearless when we're together

late-night strolls

  enduring your latest obsessions

showing you a book I love

 getting cozy in cold weather

counting our blessings

finding treasures in our storage unit

knowing just what to say

a shared life

rushing out to the dance floor
   when our song comes on

a soft touch

giving you my undivided attention

staring into your eyes

a fun double date

always making time to
see each other

falling asleep at the same time

growing your own little garden

imagining spending the
rest of our lives together

discovering your
hidden talents

fireside chats

sharing the same interests

helping you find your
keys ... again

misbehaving once in a while

freedom

adding special touches
to our house

knowing you're always
just a phone call away

a party for two

flashing a grin to
diffuse a situation

slowing down to enjoy the view

not having a care
in the world

getting lost in an
activity together

making you something

thanking you for something
I often take for granted

coming home to a big smile
after a hard day at work

playing hooky
together

putting old photos in an album
and reliving every moment

getting a package
from you

when I catch you looking at me

when plans are
canceled and we
get to stay in

dressing up in a
couple's costume

making up after
a bad fight

taking off on an
adventure

letting you relax
while I clear up

reflecting back

realizing I am completely
and utterly in love

giving you the
biggest slice

a fondue night

hearing your car
pulling up outside

bugging you when
you're grumpy

late-night snacking

an impromptu picnic

taking a rest when you need it

writing our initials in the sand

buying a souvenir to remember the trip

just walking along in silence

loving the sound of your laugh

Sandy & Danny

being in sync

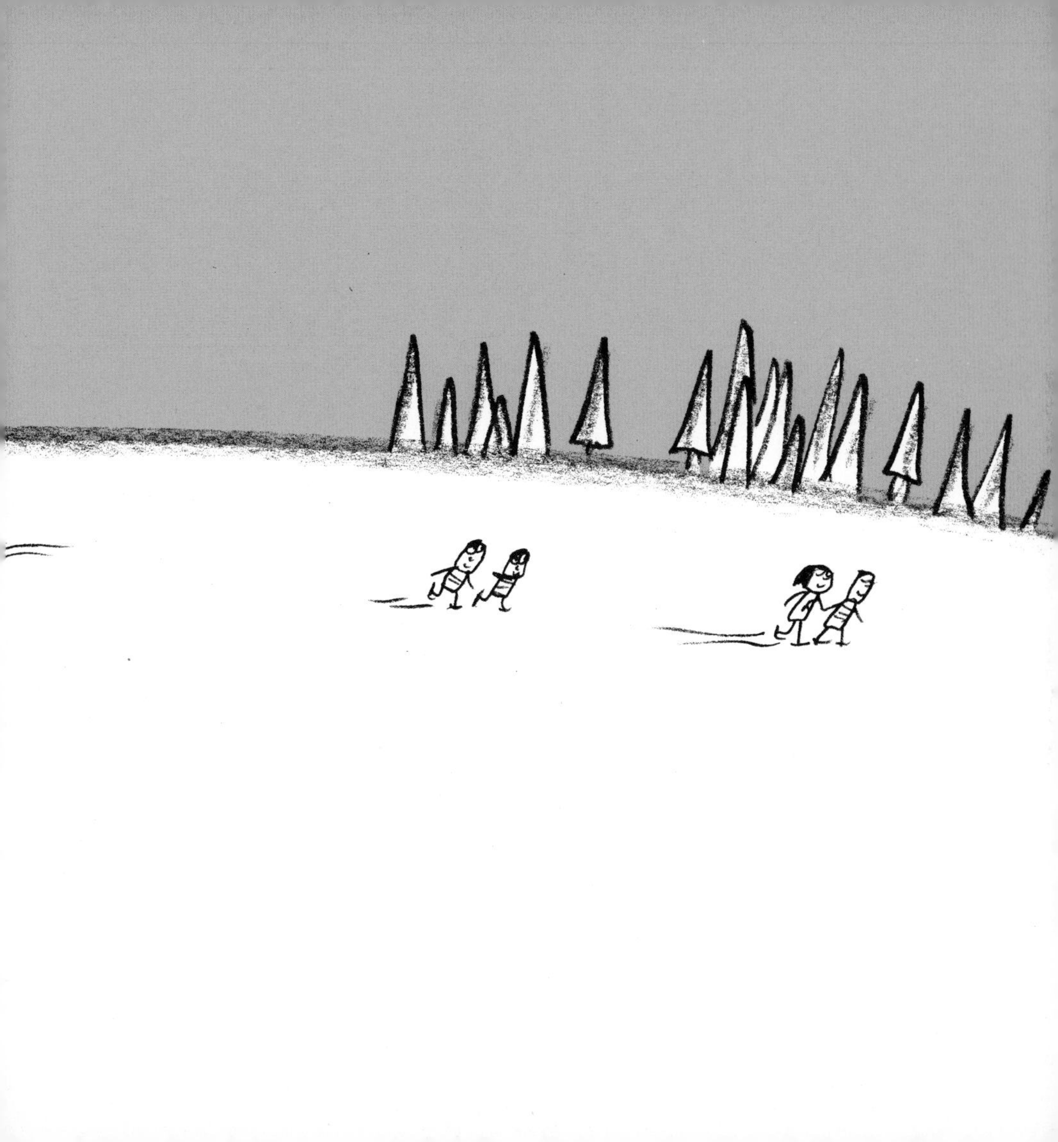

having fun

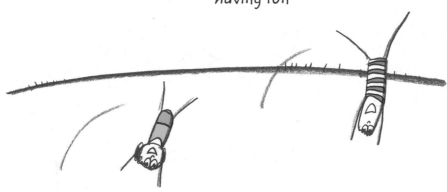

finding the perfect card for you

spending the whole
day together

being spontaneous

a comfortable silence
among all the chatter

taking wild
rides together

picking a flower for you

picking you up at the airport

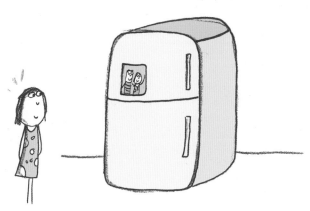

a photo of us on the fridge

taking the trip of a lifetime

a long coastal drive

walking
arm in
arm

mending a rift

sharing a
suitcase

bringing you a box
of chocolates for no
reason in particular

setting up camp

concocting
your favorite
beverage

going along with your
crazy plans

being together
in any weather

jumping in

working as a team

heading out together with no destination

getting to know you

loving your weird relatives

a romantic
getaway

being first to apologize

dressing up just for you

an emotional reunion

 seeing how cute you are in the morning

 saying yes

 buying our first car

never letting life get between us

inviting you into my family

checking off our
bucket list

riding a bicycle
built for two

getting caught in the rain

looking at photos
from when we
first met

wishing upon a star
together

ensuring you're nice
and warm

John & Yoko

making you laugh so hard you
spit out your drink

a tight hug after a
heated argument

trying new foods together

raising a family

telling you that you're the best thing that ever happened to me

knowing each other's thoughts

the sound of you breathing

when you insist on walking on the
traffic side of the sidewalk

saying "I love you" for the first time

bragging about your accomplishments

an eskimo kiss

feeling blessed to have you

escaping for the day

feeling comfortable with
you no matter what

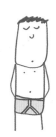

the smell of your hair

a toast in a
magical setting

making you a cake

going over the top
to amuse you

helping each other over obstacles

making promises

our silly little rituals

being celebrated
as a couple

having fun just
doing errands
together

getting each other safely to the other side

sleeping late

going for it

rereading
your old
messages

seeing you get a tad jealous

loving the same team

feeling protected

telling the story of how we met

heading
in the same direction

just chillin'

getting that little something off your cheek

framing our important pictures

laughing at stupid reality shows

telling you what I
admire about you

five minutes of
extra snuggle time

being us!

when you bat your
eyelashes

Je t'aime

saying "I love you"
in another language

reconnecting after
being apart

starting the day in
a positive way

letting you win

finding a treat
you've left me

a really
good kiss

not being afraid to
show my feelings

a special night out

harvesting what we planted

the snort you do
when laughing

knowing that we're
in this together

making you
something by hand

taking charge
of our lives

watching the world go by,
and thinking of you

reminiscing

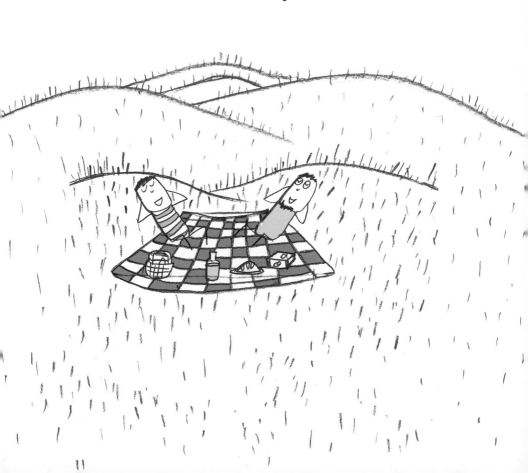

little acts of chivalry

celebrating in style

knowing I'm going to
see you later

Saturday adventures

loving our mutual friends

reading the paper
together for hours

being on cloud nine

tolerating your fashion sense

being inspired by your
example

a lazy Sunday

the turning point
between a friendship
and a relationship

getting equally enthusiastic
about fancy cheese

accepting
imperfections

playing the same tune

a feeling of awe
when we're together

booking our dream trip

making sure our life's one big adventure

tolerating your musical aspirations

a great meal with our family

leaning on
each other

helping you have more fun

going the extra mile to
make things special

having a bun
in the oven

riding the ups and downs

being in our own little world

sharing nature's wonder

admiring your originality

feeling totally content when you're home

not minding your little
mood swings

tossing away our
worries

wearing matching
jammies

a long beach walk

distracting you

loving the way you
describe things

knowing we have it really good

acting like total
nutcases for no
reason in particular

getting books for you
from the library

making your happiness
my priority

a wish that comes true

having fun in the dark

being regulars
at the local
pub

never running out of things
to talk about

jumping as high as we can

hanging out
in our pj's

giving you gentle guidance

a promise for
forever

warming each
other's feet with
our own

being able to let it all hang out

being impressed
by your genius

taking care of you when you're sick

a movie date

Tarzan & Jane

feeling like anything
is possible

sneaking up on you

your wonderful silliness

making the house nice just for you

still dating even when
we're married

being
unconventional

Antony &
Cleopatra

happy domesticity

keeping you entertained

sharing holidays with you

tolerating each other's midlife crises

waiting for you to get home

having the same
obsessions

making a life-changing
decision together

knowing I can tell you anything

having special secrets

seeing you in our kids

having a soak
together

mastering the
balancing act

239

when what we think, what we say,
and what we do are in harmony

finishing
each other's
sentences

sharing headphones

feeling the
warmth of
your hand

a stolen kiss

breakfast in bed

experimenting
in the kitchen
together

laughing at your
dumb jokes

dreaming about you,
then waking up smiling

sharing a milestone anniversary

sticking together against the odds

a goodnight kiss

when you're helpful
without being asked

a madcap adventure

having the same priorities

feeling valued

fitting together
like puzzle pieces

Rachel & Ross

going out late,
just the two of us

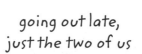

saving the last piece
of chocolate for you

watching our
wedding video

talking for hours even though we've spent all day together

when you don't want to let go

slowing down to smell the roses

taking much-needed time off

FLIGHT-1105
BARBADOS

Elizabeth Bennet
& Mr. Darcy

being proud
of your
achievements

recharging our
batteries together

knowing your taste

being partners
for life

dancing around
the house

surprising you with your
favorite meal

falling in love

seizing the moment

sharing a meal with a view

loving the song you
recommended

when you look into my
eyes that way

accepting your apology

the way you hug

having compassion

being with you in the kitchen

watching you dance

a spa day for two

feeling cool when we're together

knowing we are together in this big, vast world

pulling each other out of the hole,
no matter how deep it gets

being swept away

a spontaneous
head scratch

shared indulgences

cheering you up
when you're just at
the end of a sulk

making plans for just us!

goofing around

exploring the world

exchanging little gifts

sharing a pot of tea

admitting you were right all along

remembering when
we were younger

understanding that love
is all we need

ISBN 978-1-4521-5202-8
Manufactured in China.

FSC
www.fsc.org
MIX
Paper from
responsible sources
FSC® C008047

Design by Lisa Swerling and Ralph Lazar

10 9 8 7 6 5 4 3 2 1

Chronicle Books LLC
680 Second Street
San Francisco, CA 94107
www.chroniclebooks.com